"Park Bench Collection"

A collection of Prose, Poetry, and Art by

Roy Camblin

Roy™ Studios & Gallery

San Francisco
Paris

iUniverse, Inc.
Bloomington

"Park Bench Collection"
A Collection of Prose, Poetry, and Art

iUniverse books may be ordered through booksellers or by contacting:

iUniverse
1663 Liberty Drive
Bloomington, IN 47403
www.iuniverse.com
1-800-Authors (1-800-288-4677)

ISBN: 978-1-4502-8273-4 (sc)
ISBN: 978-1-4502-8274-1 (ebk)

Printed in the United States of America

Library of Congress Control Number: 2010918930

iUniverse rev. date: 1/3/2011

This body of work spans more than forty years and is dedicated to friends and lovers everywhere...and to Jane my partner and muse for most of those years.

Roy

Kwang Ju Letters

Sunday and having to work. The day went painfully slow, still, I was surprised at how early darkness found me.

Dinner of two beers and half a pizza at the bar with people I normally wouldn't call close friends, but just now I need their company greatly. They help take my mind off you...for maybe twenty minutes anyway. Still, you hang there in the shadows watching over me. The talk is idle and my mood is pensive. I can't really be entertained, knowing there are so many miles between us and you are too many days away to start counting down the time. Tomorrow, and tomorrow, and tomorrow, I will arise and do what is expected of me. Then suddenly it will all be over and there will be just six hours of flying time between us, and that will be the hardest time of all, when every minute is an eternity, and nothing will drive you from my most immediate thoughts.

Kwang Ju, too far south for snow this early, but very much in winter's grasp. The night air crisp...by morning the puddles will be laced with ice, the mud as hard as stone. Taking in the evening air, under a cold, clear winter sky filled with bright stars, I could think of little else but you. No direction to my thoughts, just an arabesque of feelings that you've brought to me, a delicate arrangement of our favorite dreams, so easily upset by life's intrusion, but always coming into balance when we're alone together making love.

And the days, brown days with rust brown mud and all the buildings the same rust brown color. The grass along the roads, the rice paddies, and the last few leaves that refuse to fall...all brown. There's not a bit of color anywhere, save a hazy gray sky that provides some relief. But in the morning and early evening, even the sky turns the same rust brown. It's a red-brown world this strange place called Korea and it has taken me from you.

Only one day gone, and I know this will be a very lonely time. What will I do when you're a week away? I couldn't bear a year. Watching the young men drifting into town, I saw none filled with any hope or aspiration, just lonely men on solitary errands, going out to barter for one night of love at a time.

How lucky I feel to have you. Ever constant, ever present, I need nothing else. Just knowing what you've been to me is enough. How dear you've become. I cannot talk of loving you just now or surely I will cry.

The Asian mind; deliberate people; each person with a purpose and a place; no station in life too low; every task worth doing; that strange, unique oriental combination of humility and pride...these are priceless people.

It's been another long day of waiting. There is one thing left out of yesterday that I feel is worth recalling. The area between the runway and taxiway at Kwang Ju is a large marsh with wild rice growing in and around the water. Sitting on a dike in the middle of this marsh is the mobile control unit that I drove out to inspect before dark. I had been standing there a short while, lost in thoughts of you, feeling very much alive in the early evening chill, filled with a peace that no Sunday afternoon had provided in a long time, wondering how you were and what you were doing, when the marsh birds came. Three great skeins of ducks that circled the marsh once and all came down one, two, or half a dozen at a time to settle on the water around me. I was fixed with fascination. Afraid to move, that I might spoil the vision.

There's no explaining the joy that filled me, and the anguish I suffered because you weren't there to share it...knowing no words could recount the beauty of that moment, feeling somehow I'd cheated you having had such a vision that was not ours together. Silly I know, but that's how much I love you. Scold me if you will for being so closed, but loving you less would be impossible.

We live a short-order life. You are my days and nights, my springtime, summer, winter, fall...you are my every season, my reason for believing. You are my source of dreams. Sleep well my lady, you are much loved.

(As the water from a spring pours out upon the earth and surrounds itself with life and beauty, so have you found your way into my soul, and made for me a garden in an otherwise dry and wasted world.)

It's getting close to coming home, and sitting down to write isn't easy anymore. Seems all I have to do is hold my breath just one more night (maybe two) and I'll find myself within the safety of your arms again. Will you save Sunday for me, and Monday too? Maybe there will be enough of Saturday left to start the painful process of getting reacquainted. The hours go so quickly when we're in bed.

In the beginning there was me, in the end when all is said and done, there will be only me...but in between there is you, and that is more than I could have ever hoped for.

Journey

I walked a long way
Today,
Talked a long time
To Say,
What didn't matter
Anyway,
That I love you
Every way.

Find a way
This day,
Love me more
Your way.

I went out one day,
And never came back.
She came home the same day
To stay.

Coming or going,
My timing's been bad.
Try as I may,
That's the luck I've had.

Supper's On

There are some things in love
You can't demand.
You can get your dinner on time;
Get your rocks off twice a week,
Even if she isn't in the mood.
But that cherished warmth
That comes late at night,
Or those small expressions
Of pride in all you do
And who you are,
These things come
From giving,
Giving first,
In full measure
Honestly.

How

How sweet your mouth
How telling your eyes
How beautiful your mind
How steady your love
How great my need
How unworthy I.

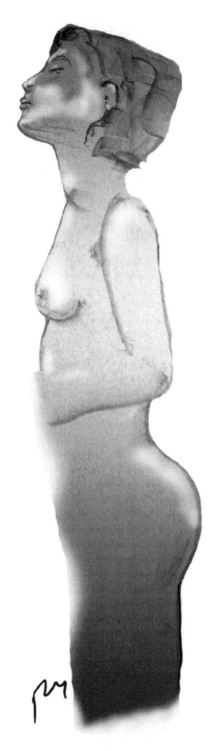

Unspoken

There is no moment
Between my wakening
And my sleeping
That is not filled
With you.

We carry on
So many conversations
In my thinking
That when we're together
It's all been said.

And so
We spend our time
Making love
And the words
Are never necessary.

14

Old Faces

What junkyard of the mind
Accumulates and stores
Such memories?
Perishables, deep frozen
In forgotten larders;
Defrosted in the autumn years
Of increasing disappointment
And failing health
For bare subsistence.

In those last days
Of final winter,
When it's only...
Only the memories that serve,
Or come to visit,
Or care,
Or whisper softly in the night.

No one asks to be old.
I cannot pass today
One more of those vacant faces,
Without at least
Stopping to say
Hello!

Siege

This war locked city
Shroud in cloud
Grayest morning
Of my lifetime
So far away,
Your light.
Bend your thoughts to me,
Divide this Sea Of Silence
Like Moses split the Red.
Cross over to me now
For all of Pharaoh's armies
Are upon me
And I am at great need.

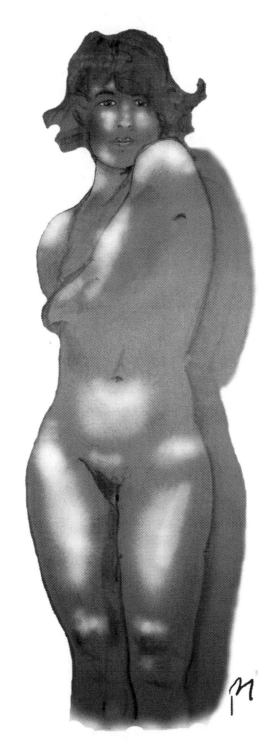

Insomnia

Small voices
That follow through the night,
Robbing dreams
And making sleep
Impossible.

What form of light
Will drive you from
The darkened corners
Of my room
And return peace
To this tortured mind?

Self Denial

Timid heart tremble
At loves attention,
Though void of sorrow.
Shallow chalice of virtue
You hold so little.

Who Says?

Who was it that said
Tomorrow will bring nothing new?
Wasn't it you?
Do you think you're the same
As when we met?
And will you be the same
When I am gone?
Someone will come along
And surely change you.

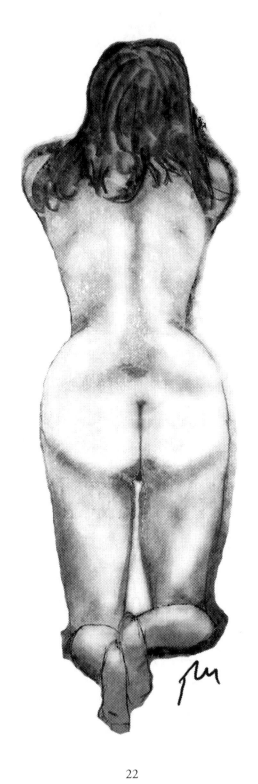

On Good Beginnings

So many people go through life
Looking for promises of happy endings,
Passing up what could have been
A few good beginnings.

Thank you for taking a chance with me.
You could have passed me by,
So very long ago.

We start out after life,
And the first thing you know,
We are chasing after
Something else.

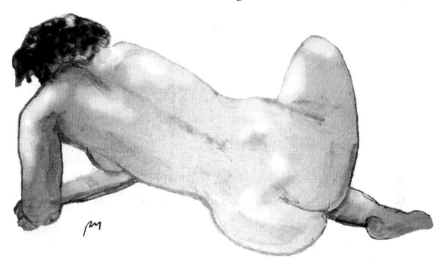

Endings

People look for happy endings when they should be looking for good
beginnings. I've gone through a lot of beginnings, but still haven't found
my ending. Maybe that's the way it should be.

Middle-Aged Love Affair

Gray lady, my middle life lover
How mellow are your moods.
Haven of life's pleasures,
Resurrection of my childhood,
You are my one true friend.

Rendezvous

It came and went *so* quickly...
Time cheats us.
But we can beat him at his own game
Stealing moments from his clock;
And days from his calendar
The banquet of a whole night together...

And *touching...*!
When time isn't watching...

Winter Whispers

Quietly I move about,
Listening to the soft murmur
Of conversation
From the room next door.
Lovers...At the window
I watch a raindrop
Moving down the glass,
Merge with another,
Each losing its identity;
Continuing down,
Only to be lost
In some oblivion
At the bottom of the pain.

The park beyond,
Wrapped in gray,
Where the bare bones of trees
Stand watch for Spring.
Their Spring will come again.
If life's seasons could
Repeat themselves...
But for us,
Spring comes but once.

Night Sweat

You may think
That throbbing rush
Coursing in your neck
And mind
And breast,
Felt through all your limbs
Is just your heart.
It's not...it's mine;
Beating for you
Half a world away.

Would that I were the wind
To grace your wings and be
In flight with you tonight,
Sharing some small peace
Of earth and sky...
Called heaven.

Friends

(Written to the author)

Though they were very dissimilar in character,
They also shared many tastes and appetites,
And those they didn't share
They tolerated in one another with instinctive respect,
As a necessary spice of difference.

They knew each other very well indeed...
His natural tendency was to deplore human failings in others
And ignore them in himself.
Her natural tendency was to understand
And forgive human failings in others,
And be merciless upon them in herself.

He felt himself invincibly strong;
She knew herself perilously weak;
And somehow it all came together
As a nearly perfect friendship,
In the name of which
Nothing was impossible.

Out Of Time

This won't be finished now.
The wind is up...and...
I fear the tempest.
If rejection is upon me,
There will be little comfort
In yesterdays remembered.
I hold my breath
And wait.

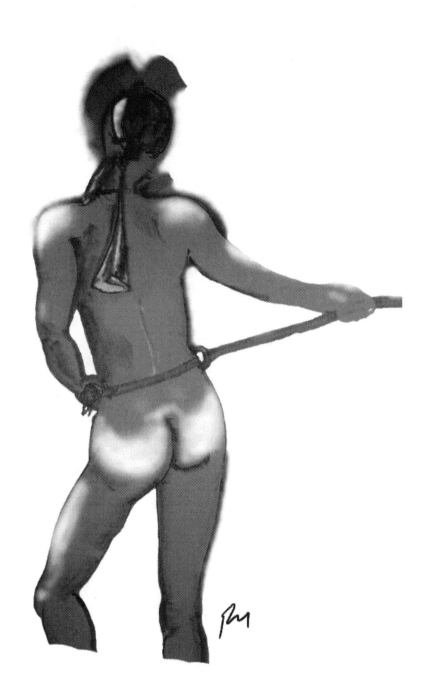

Breaking Up

How easily we don't remember...
I know someone had to be
The last one out the door.
I'm glad it wasn't you, but God,
I wish it didn't have to be me!
I still need your needing me.

I know that in time you will deal
With these past few years in your own way;
Find a purpose and a place for everything
That has happened between us.
I knew the time would come
When you'd force a re-negotiation
Of our relationship.
I've been a dangling participle
In your personal life,
And you with a fondness for proper
(If not perfect) endings.

I have always had my way with you,
Until now...and now,
I know it must be your way,
To preserve that gentle heart
From too much damage.
I know there will still be
A warm, special spot for me
When you're done re-arranging
Although diminished.
I will accept that,
The penalty for inaction.
But for my part, I'll always
Love you...just as much
And more.

Epilogue

Well here we are again,
Much later,
Much older.
There's not much to be said
For quitting.
I've tried telling myself
I understand.
But you've gotten too good
At not loving me.

Loose Ends

Picking up loose ends,
Trying to piece back together
That most precious of experiences.
I'll love you less passionately now,
With reason,
In your season,
At your times.

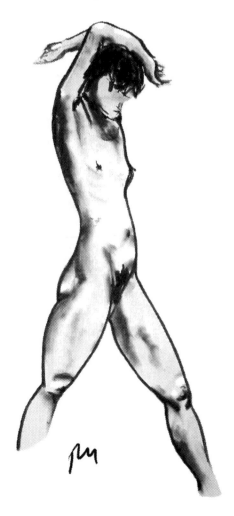

Promise

First flower of this new season
First blossom to follow winter's thaw
Spring's promise
Of so much more.

I've learned so much from you
That I knew before
But had forgotten.

More On Promises

We kiss frogs because
We're promised Princes.
All I've ever gotten
Is an occasional wart.

Love Affair

I've charted every line and shadow
Been the object of your smiles
And frowns
Been beside you when you needed
Been a part of every up
And down.

Love's Cadence

I fill the moments between seeing you
With conversations I'd have liked to have.
And there's never any time to talk
When we're alone together;
We make love desperately instead.
So let my touch talk...
Feel my longing for you
In the way my hands
Caress you face...
And neck
...and...

The way my breathing fills the dark room
With love's loud cadence.

I've spent my entire week
Working my way
Toward just these few moments
With you.

He To She...

Soft, Sad, Sensitive.
Lovely, Lonely Lady.
Warm, Wonderful Wishes.
Kind Coital Kisses.

She To He...

Tender, Timid Turtle
Too Tired To Tango.
Last Little Lover.
Late, Lean, Lewd.
Mello Minded Mood.

Metamorphosis

(Dark encounter)

Metamorphosis my moth,
Tell me of your flight.
Creepy, crawly creature;
Caterpillar's demise.
Munching twig and leaf,
You screwed yourself up tight;
Wrapped around with silken thread,
Holding out the light.
What agony you suffered
To undergo such changes?
Shedding limp and lithe your skin,
Your life style re-arranges.
Winging to nearby garden
Or far off meadow,
Now you dine on nectar sweet,
And have forgotten
Yesterday's trouble.

China, 1978

Single's Scene

Sitting at the bar for hours;
Watching other lonely people
Pairing off to face the darkening,
Thickening night.
Knowing the waiting morning
Can be too cruel,
When too much light
Shatters,
Scatters the dream
That held the night together.
Too seldom awakening with hopes in tack;
To be re-affirmed with breakfast, lunch, and dinner,
Another night together.

Still, we are driven not to be lonely.
And so,
I give up my seat
To another faceless member of the crowd,
And move toward you.
I can only say "hello" and hope.

Endangered Species

(The American Hobo)

Wide ribbon of highway,
Carrying this nation's industry
Upon its back.
Stretched such distances,
In such directions
That no man
Could travel every mile
In a single lifetime.

I know what causes me to wander;
The subtle enticement
Of just one more town;
My private seduction
Of every hillside and valley
...my love affair
With this land.

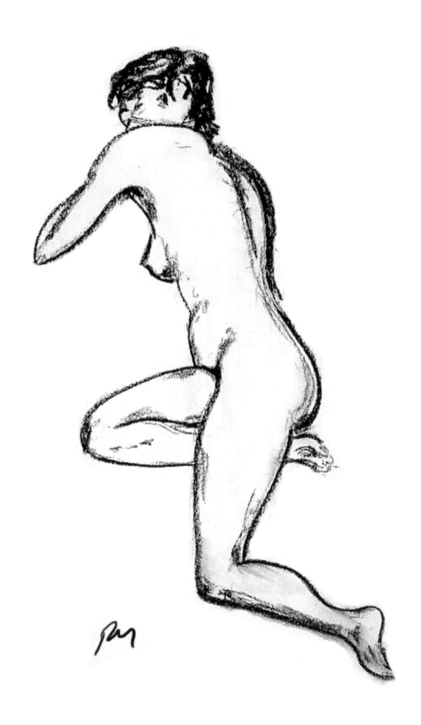

Tourist Trade

Manipulator,
Master-baiter,
Master of maidens'
Minds and morals,
Mood mender,
Mind bender,
Body lender...
How well you ply your trade
...doesn't matter,
They all go home anyway.

Well Met

I haven't walked the lonely roads
Through dirty towns
To meet this time
Without learning (at least)
A little about love
And the knowing look
I see
In your bright eyes.
I could spend a lifetime
Mapping out your mind
And still be lost
In wonder
At every turn.
Bewildered by your touch,
Your hips and thighs
Amaze me.

Perspectives

(Point and Counter Point)

Man has defaced,
Scarred and marred
That which God wrought,
With great pain
Over great time;
Made a twisted, tangled jungle
Of stone and steel
Where once trees and flowers
And green grass grew.

Ah, but he has lifted
And formed
From the earth
Things of great wonder;
Molded the earth
With his craft;
Met increasing needs
With his imagination;
Created a thing of industry
In this otherwise primitive world.

Postcard From Mike's American Bar & Grill

(10th Ave at 46th St NYC)

"The funky, down-and-dirty exterior of the Big Apple's hottest chili spot. The neighborhood, Hell's Kitchen, is suitably seedy."...reads the caption on the postcard. Mike stands out front pulling in customers off the street. I couldn't find chili on the menu, but had a great plate of jerk chicken and garlic mashed potatoes.

I took a chance the other night on this place in New York City...it was fun. Hell's Kitchen has seen two centuries of immigrants, one wave after another, occupy it's buildings for a generation then move on, turning them back to yet another arriving culture seeking refuge in this land of hope and promise. The decor in Mike's changes monthly...one man's accelerated reflection of the generational shifts of the neighborhood... seedy, but honest and rich with life. This establishment has always been an anchor point for the current tenants of those sixth floor walk-ups where men in dirty T shirts sit at the windows watching the activity on the street, as the sun sets and night begins...my pace quickens. I emerge, hours later, high in spirit, to find the neighborhood quite changed. The commuters and tourists have departed, as have their window watchers; and now the activity centers in doorways where more subdued dramas unfold. My pace slackens as I linger to eavesdrop on the quiet conversations, picking up the occasional thread of laughter, trying to unpack their lives from the few words I capture, and the occasional smile they share...

The Birds

The birds collect in the trees beside the road one-by-one.
But they take flight all at once,
Darkening the sky and beating the wind with their wings.
I cower close to the earth.
I am afraid.
They pass, and brightness returns.
I walk on, erect, but not as tall.
That moment of fear has made my Self shorter.
The shame follows me most of the day.

The birds collect in the trees beside the road one-by-one.
They take flight all at once,
Darkening the sky and beating the wind with their wings.
I stand tall and their wings beat upon my face,
But I show no fear.
They pass, and the day continues to darken,
For the world is full of storm.
I walk on, erect, taller.
The birds have prepared me for what is coming.

The following three selections are extracts from a travel
journal...Australia 1998

Tropic Nights

Evening in Cairns...with friends 11/29/98

We sat together at the table board
Long into the night
Telling stories and laughing,
Drinking red wine
And Baileys.
The only lights in the room
Were candles
And a single lamp
Throwing soft light
Against the dark wood panels.
The ceiling fan
Kept the candles dancing,
As the hot wax
Flowed lazily
Onto the table,
...as lazy as the conversation.
At last the candles guttered,
And we each made our way,
Individually,
Off to bed.
The night was hot,
And wet
I lay there in the dark
Until the sights
And sounds
And smells
Of the night left my head,
And my heart was free
To follow after you.

PS: Did I forget to mention Philip's pumpkin soup?

Sweet November

Patti worries what she'll look like...
Will the artist be kind?
You worry too much!
Lines and words come slowly.
Scattered drops before a shower...
Timid at first...
Then the deluge!

Holloway Beach...lunch...
The vine climbs the post like a centipede,
With its many attachments.
Where are you going?
Will anyone follow?

As an instrument,
You are strings,
Not keyboard.
I hope you find someone
With the art
To play you.
Your tones are mellow and deep,
You just haven't found
The right harmony.
It's out there...you must believe that,
Or there isn't any reason
To play on.

Piano Man

If he played his wife
The way he played his piano,
She'd have been a very happy woman.

Seldom right,
But never in doubt…
The world constricts around him.
They've stopped listening,
And now…
The bench is empty.

Sweet Charlotte

March 26, 1999…a letter to my friend in Fortuna California…
on her death bed

You are frequently in my thoughts and I often find myself telling others about you…the special lady who cared for my two young children and touched all our lives with her patience, wisdom, and love. You brought a certain balance to our lives at a time when it was needed, and your history became our history, and lives with us in the stories we tell and the memories we share. You are with us always, woven into our tapestry, and the tapestries of so many others you've adopted over your lifetime. All our thoughts and affections are with you.

Epilog

Charlotte Milton died on Saturday April 3rd 1999 at around 8:30pm… she was 92 years old. She died the way she lived, in total control, and with unsurpassed dignity. She simply said…enough…and the force that so animated this woman in life, simply left her body. Wherever she is now, I'm sure she's in charge. She always had a following, a constellation of souls that were always lifted by her indomitable spirit…like leaves on a fresh breeze. Charlotte, you are missed.

Just One Charlotte Story…for the road

Charlotte was the primary care giver for both my children until they entered pre-school…to them she was simply Grandma…well into her 80's. When Vikki was two, grandma went into a prolonged funk. For years she'd shown up on Thursday mornings with a certain *glow*. It happened that she was having an affair with a gentleman down on the peninsula, and Wednesday nights had always been their weekly time together. Grandma was in a funk because her companion had just died…at the age of *a hundred and five*. Apparently, this gentleman had picked Charlotte up at the slot machines in Reno…

when he was *ninety* …
and had kept her smiling for the intervening *fifteen* years!
I raise my glass to both of them…wherever they may be.

Two Mirrors...Facing

RE: a smile...your smile...
Reflecting my smile...
      Reflecting your smile...
          And so it repeats...
              And compounds...
                  To infinity.
Thus we illustrate the boundlessness of love,
An endless illusion of widening ripples that recede into,
      Not across,
What our senses tell us can only be
A two dimensional space,
The natural discord between head and heart
...I love you.

You Are Always On My Mind

From the beginning,
We were bound together
With comfortable lies,
The cultures of our childhoods,
Upon which
Nothing substantial could be built.

Now we are bound together
By the discovery of painful truths,
And suddenly all things become possible.

We stand again on love's threshold,
With renewed thrust and passion,
Rediscovering shared needs and values.
True fidelity becomes probable,
And nothing seems beyond our grasp.

Welcome Home

A morning thought
To lubricate
The grinding moments
In your day...

I have no religion
In the conventional sense,
But I belief profoundly
In what we have together
...now.

Making love to you
Is the closest I've ever come
To communion with a Greater Whole.
I am fractional without you.

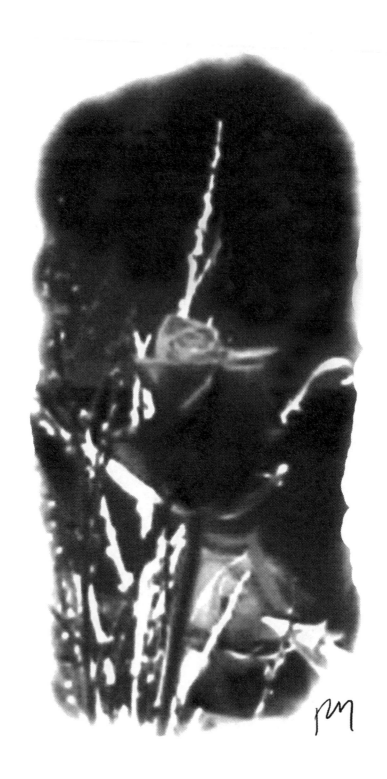

Drawing Blood

The Rose
Never apologizes
For *her* thorns.
And there is pain
Buried
In *her* pleasures,
But that's what makes a Rose
a Rose.

I am not a Rose
And must apologize
For *my* thorns.
I only want
You to feel
My profound love
Not the thorny
…prick.

Letters From The Road

I was deeply saddened
By the turn our conversation
Took today.
Your anger is a widening ocean
With so many tributaries;
I don't pretend to understand
Where it comes from.
I just know I love you
...unconditionally.
I reach out tonight with an olive branch,
Each leaf a photo of my time in Sundance.
I will keep a photo journal
Of my winter here to share with you
When you return from Paris in the spring.
You are a special lady.
I will hold the tender times in my head
And close to my heart
To get beyond the pain of the day
And find sleep tonight.

On Having a Fire Goddess For A Muse

The good muse
Relaxes with the musing…
And finds _a_musement
In the fumbling words
Of her poet,
Knowing too critical an eye
Will cause word and thought
To retreat
And inspiration
To vanish.

I will anticipate
Your kindness
Toward all I endeavor,
And will produce
Uncommon works
Of introspection
Out of love…
For you.

Mortally yours,

Married Man

Any Port In A Storm

A great emptiness fills this house
When you're not here.
We don't speak of it...
We try not to name it...
Because giving it thought
Only makes it more horrible,
And the time without you
That must be endured
Moves more slowly.

A great darkness fills me
When I am abandoned.
I utter no word
Or have no thought
That is not of you...
The horror
Of your gathering distance
Grows daily
And darkens my thoughts.
Loneliness and doubt
Are my constant companions
And they harass me
Without mercy.
I must find safe harbor
Before the dawn
Or I will founder
In this storm...

On Broken Homes

The children always pay the price. My oldest son, the product of a prior marriage, who I long felt was lost to me, though I tried to keep pace with his life in the two decades of his growing up through weekly phone calls and once or twice yearly visitations...never enough. The visits got shorter and less frequent as the demands of his separate life encroach on our time with him...a new girlfriend, football camp, a special holiday with his mom. The list of conflicting priorities grew longer as his life as a young adult took shape. I can remember a discussion with a female co-worker when divorce was only just being contemplated. She was from a broken home and remembered how miserable her summers had been because she and her siblings had to spend that time with their dad. They loved him and he was a good father, but it meant not being with friends or sharing the same prospects of summer that made the pending conclusion of each school year so momentous. It also meant not having the same summer experiences as their friends, and starting the next school year isolated and alone...new summer alliances having been formed to the exclusion of past friendships. This co-worker's sympathies and lamentations were definitely with my son, who was not yet three years old. I vowed at the time to never be in conflict with my son's reasonable desires regarding where he spent his vacations, and he rewarded us with his love and the periodic visits that benchmarked our lives and the passage of years. I can also be thankful that whatever her personal feeling toward me, his mother was reasonable and always encouraged his relationship with me and my second family. If my relationship with him was less than it could have been, the failure was mine...not hers or his or theirs. I was still learning to be a parent.

Your Paparazzi

Here I sit in front of a blank screen
Wondering how to collect my thoughts
In a way to let you know I care,
To amuse and delight you.

Like a writer with a blank sheet of paper
The empty screen stares back at me,
But like a snow field,
Slowly yields its secrets
As the eyes adjust to the glare.

And what do I see she asks?
The Polaroid of our brief friendship
Patiently taking form before us,
Gaining more clarity and color
With each passing moment,
The smiles that break upon our faces
As we see ourselves...together!
Let's take another...
And another...
Until we've filled every shelf and drawer
With a lifetime of memories.
Each snapshot of a special time together
Adds another pearl on the necklace
That becomes our life.

Exerts from an unpublished novel **<u>Millennium</u>**
By Roy Camblin, all rights reserved
Book One

Retrospect...One Man's Journey

John Chambers, CEO of the biggest bank in the world. Deal maker, political savant, a very worn-out man one week into a two week vacation in Portugal with the children from both his marriages. It's Sunday, June 29th. The children are awakened at 6am by pounding on the door. It's the local constabulary looking for John Chambers. The policeman speaks very little English, but gets across that there's an urgent message to call the American Embassy. He gives John two poorly transcribed numbers; neither looks like a valid phone number. Pulling on shorts and a shirt, John heads out into the cool morning to find a phone. The MCI operator tries various combinations of the numbers, both for the US and Europe, but without results. He shrugs it off and he heads back to the villa.

Barely back in bed, there's pounding on the door again. This time it's the estate agent who manages the property they've rented. John pulls on cloths again and greets him in the yard.

"Are you John Chambers?"

"I am."

"There's a family emergency. You need to come down to my office. There's a Richard Harrison at the US Embassy trying to reach you."

It's only minutes to the office. He opens up, gives instruction on how to dial the number, and withdraws to the street outside where he lights up a smoke. John dials the number and waits for an answer.

"Hello, I'm John Chambers. I've received a message that a Richard Harrison is trying to reach me."

"Yes, this is Richard Harrison. I'm the duty officer here at the American Embassy. Mr. Chambers, your sister has been trying to reach you since Friday. I regret to inform you that your brother Fred was killed in an auto accident. I don't have any further details, but you can reach your sister in Denver at (303) 211-2739."

John thanks him and then calls his sister. The story he's told doesn't make sense, something about his brother falling out of his car on the way to work and then being run over by a minivan. John agrees to get to Denver as fast as he can to help sort things out. His corporate jet could be waiting at Faro within a few hours, but instead he decides to take the four hour cab ride to Lisbon and make commercial connections to Denver. He needs time on a slower track to absorb the news of his brother's death, reflect, and think. If he called the office he'd be sucked back into all the problems they were dealing with when he left. He could already feel the office's gravitational pull with the first knock on the door that morning.

It's after 6 pm by the time John finally gets away, but the sun is still high in a clear summer sky. The cab leaves the coast at Carwarro and heads inland through Lagos toward Sevils. It's a comfortable Mercedes, picked by John from a line of cabs because it is covered with no smoking signs. The driver speaks little English, but they'll get by. Almost immediately the passing game begins. The Portuguese are suicidal drivers. The roads are narrow and most drivers aren't licensed. They have the worst driving statistics in Europe. They drive fast in large packs playing leap frog passing, passing, passing, They pass on curves, on bridges, into on-coming traffic, frequently four abreast on two lane roads with no shoulders and limited sight distance.

On a few close calls, the driver falls back and gives way. Good! He just might have some brains. John loosens his seat belt a little and settles back, watching the landscape slip by, green rolling hills with red soil, covered in small orchards of nuts and citrus trees. Whitewashed Mediterranean houses with red tiled roofs are clustered on the hill tops surrounded by vineyards. Most have become summer Villas for British or German ex-patriots.

It will be a long journey, without the corporate comforts he's become accustomed to. His mood is dark and pensive. Grieving will come later. For now, the chapters of his past lives begin rolling through his mind, transitioning from one chapter to the next with changes in the passing landscape. It's a time for critical thinking, each memory being put in the balance for self judgment. How can Fred be dead at 43? How will the world ever be the same without his sense of humor, his laughter? How can 16 years of marriage be melting away on a beach in the Algarve, like a sand castle in the surf…and he can't seem to do anything about it.

***

John was the oldest of seven children; three boys, four girls. Now there would only be six. Fred was born in Virginia on December 27th 1953, the fourth child. They were service brats, third generation military. The family had lived in Texas, Georgia, Florida, California, Japan, Kentucky, Virginia, Turkey, South Carolina, Alabama, Oregon, Delaware, Korea, Nevada, Arizona, Philippines, Hawaii, and Florida again, by the time John left home for college. They were nomads without roots or geography.

A generation of Military men lost their lives, not in battles through acts of courage defending their country, but in slow, private battles with a culture that glamorized alcohol…open bar at lunch, nickel drinks at happy hour, even the flying safety meetings were held at the bar. In the early years, John's parents were a virile, happy couple, often entertaining, frequently celebrating advancements in his father's career; gentle and caring with their children…life was good. John was in the fifth grade in Charleston South Carolina when the spankings became more than nominal, and his mother would frequently be found crying in the kitchen, with a dinner getting cold and not knowing whether to wait for their father to come home from the bar or to go ahead and feed the children. Either way she would be on the receiving end of his wrath. Happy Hours weren't happy any more. John was in the seventh grade, living in Montgomery Alabama, the first time he witnessed his father hitting his mother. By eighth grade, his father would stalk the house looking for any excuse to go into a rage. John, as the oldest was usually the grounding point for his father's wrath. Beatings were frequent, typically being knocked down in the bottom of a closet and kicked then pummeled with fists, or knocked backward out of his chair at the dinner table. Meal time was always the worst…that was Portland Oregon. His mother had been a talented artist, but seven children and being married to an alcoholic had made her old and tired by forty. She got sucked into the same vortex his father was caught in.

John spent most of his teenage years raising his siblings and being their protector; getting them fed, dressed and off to school in the morning; fed, cleaned-up and into bed at night; helping them with their homework; sharing his bed with a little one if they were hurt or frightened. From the age of ten he was working, taking any odd job he could find to accumulate money, putting shoes on their feet for the beginning of school, if they had none, playing Santa on Christmas Eve from the fifth grade on, ensuring that everyone always had something under the tree on Christmas morning. John was the center of their young universe and they hung together with him in a pack, fiercely defensive of one another, supporting each other with a strength and love that was tempered daily. Summers and weekends they'd spend in the fields surrounding the house, lost in adventure, following John as their captain. The youngest siblings were still in bottles and diapers, but they were part of the gang and went everywhere with John. They were their own tribe.

But John abandoned them when he was eighteen. It was not intentional, but the currents of life swept him away and it would be ten long years before they'd all be back together again. Fred assumed the role of protector and leader after John was gone. He became the new tribal captain, and paid a dear price with their father. Their parent's condition continued to worsen.

By the time John was eighteen home life had a definite pattern. His parents' drinking on the weekends started late morning, with his father's escalating belligerence through the afternoon, culminating in a rage and physical abuse, then his father passing out before dinner on the living room rug in his under wear. On this particular Sunday afternoon, they were faced off in the kitchen, John interceding for one of his younger sisters. His father was in a rage after finding a safety razor that she had left on the side of the bathtub. There was his father's usual shouting, then the fists. But on this occasion, John grabbed his father around the chest and hugged him roughly, pressing his face into his father's, holding his arms down and saying over and over "Dad, we love you...dad, we love you!" From that moment forward, his father had no power over John.

In later years there would be an unspoken pride and understanding between them, but that would come much later. John moved out of his father's house the following day. He had no contact with the family for the next ten years, something he would often regret.

John supported himself through his last year in high school working the beaches and fishing boats around Panama City, couch surfing at the homes of friends who would take him in, at least for a night or two. He excelled in sports, graduated with honors, got the highest score on his SAT tests, and had his choice of colleges. But he was financially strapped, so instead he worked his way across the south, unloading freight cars, working in warehouses, painting billboards along the nation's highways, washing dishes in grubby diners, anything he could find, including three years as a circus performer under the second largest tent in the world. Vietnam and the draft eventually pushed him back toward college. He graduated in 1969 with a degree in Marketing and a commission in the Air Force. He met his first wife that same summer. They spent a year in Las Vegas, and then moved to Phoenix where John went through pilot training.

In 1972, the state of Florida removed the last three children from his parent's home and placed them in foster care. John found out about it three weeks later, and within 48 hours had his two youngest sisters flown to Phoenix to join him. They were 11 and 14, not the children in bottles and diapers that he'd remembered. John became their legal guardian and raised them through high school. His youngest brother was only in tenth grade, but elected to stay on his own, supporting himself much the way John had years earlier. Fred though was lost. He'd left home several years earlier when the family was back in Korea, and no one had seen or heard from him since.

***

John is jolted back into the moment by the passing game. The driver is getting more aggressive now, and he's lit a cigarette. John taps at one of the no smoking signs and gestures for the driver to put it out. Suddenly the driver speaks *no* English and shows no understanding; just keeps shrugging and waving his hands in the air, mumbling something in Portuguese...*stupid American!*

John opens a window. His mood darkens further; now he's mad. Brooding, all the storm clouds of his life seem to have gathered for this journey. The landscape has changed again. There are more eucalyptus trees lining the roads now; tall and majestic, creating covered canyons for the pack of passing cars to lunge through, sucked forward, each blind curve or on-coming stream of trucks causing a frenzy of last moment passing, Lemmings rushing to their deaths.

***

John spent his first year in the service as a supply officer at the Air Force's Top Gun School outside of Las Vegas. The ultimate scrounger and deal maker, he could find a way to get anything done. He'd been denied a chance to become a pilot because his eyes weren't perfect. He worked hard that first year, got a Major General's endorsement on his latest application, and three weeks later he at last had orders for pilot training. Because he had prior service and higher date of rank than his class mates, he ended up as the Student Flight Commander. In addition to getting himself through a grueling 48 week program, he was responsible for getting 81 other officers through as well. This was 1970; the height of the Vietnam air war and the Air Force's pilot training program had been compressed from 52 weeks into 48, with no reduction in requirements. It had devolved into a dog-eat-dog wash-out program with every student stepping on one another to get the top spots and their choice of aircraft assignments. The instructors fed the competitive frenzy and maintaining a sustained level of hazing that made for a miserable year. As a result, the prior class had had an elimination rate of over 60%, many self initiated.

John arrived the month prior to the beginning of the program to get a sense for what lay ahead, and decided this wasn't the way he wanted to spend the next year of his life. It didn't have to be this way. He wasn't going to play by their rules. As his classmates arrived, John and his wife spent time doing early bonding and team building. Over the first few weeks John instilled his own program of 'cooperate and graduate', generating a genuine group concern for one another. He set up help groups, persuading top performers to help those in trouble, and ensured that no one in the class fell too far behind. Forty-eight weeks later his class graduated 79 out of 81 officers that had begun the program together. Of the remaining two, one had had pneumonia; the other broke a leg during parachute training. Both completed the program with a later class. Ten years later the Air Force did a study on John's class. As a group, they had had the best safety record ever, and the Air Force wanted to know why. What was their finding? An anomaly, it couldn't be explained. For John, the year provided several pivotal lessons: if you don't like the rules, you have the power to change them. You can be more powerful and effective working behind the spotlight than in it...**if** your focus is on achievement, not credit.

After graduation, John was plowed back into the pilot training program as a T-38 instructor teaching advanced flight techniques in high performance jets. That only lasted a year, before he got tagged for an assignment in Thailand flying F-4C Wild Weasels, whose mission was to detect and destroy radar guided missile sites in North Vietnam. John went through F-4C certification and Weasel training enroot and arrived at Udorn Air Base in mid December 1971. He met his back seater, a weapons officer named Dan Squires, who was on his second tour in South East Asia. Together they went through the local orientation program and logged their first combat mission on Christmas Day.

Most combat aircrew losses occurred in the first six weeks of arrival in theater. There were periods when losses were as high as one in three of the new arrivals. However, if you survived the first six weeks, there was a reasonable probability that you'd make it home when your twelve months were over. It was mid January, John and Dan were part of a two-ship formation, Red Flight, headed north over the DMZ for a mission just southwest of Hanoi. Hank and Sandy were the pilot and weapons officer respectively in the other aircraft. The normal flight profile was to fly to the designated target area in a loose 'fluid wing', which allowed four sets of eyes to scan both the ground for missiles or cannon fire, and the air for enemy aircraft. It's always what you don't see that gets you. The target for the day was a set of mobile SA6 missile launchers that aerial reconnaissance had photographed in new ground emplacements protecting one of the primary bombing corridors into Hanoi's industrial district. Approaching the target area, the flight would separate and the lead, called the 'eyeball', would make a high-speed run over the target area. The objective was to get the mobile launchers to turn on their active radar and lock onto the first aircraft. The second aircraft, called the 'shooter', would hang back at a distance and fire one or more HARM missiles, which fix on the active radar and home in on the site. After the radar is knocked out, the pair of F-4Cs then drop canisters of cluster bombs on the site, effectively taking out any personnel, missiles, or trucks that weren't destroyed by the HARM missiles.

Their run on the target had been text book. The pair of Weasels re-joined south of the target and headed away from Hanoi for the DMZ. They were climbing through 10,000 feet when the threat warning panels in both aircraft lit up like Christmas trees, and almost immediately there was a loud blaring in the headsets indicating lock-on and launch of an enemy surface-to-air missile.

"Shit!" echoed in both cockpits.

"Red Flight, hard left!", John called out over the radio, his voice already straining under a 9G, 90 degree banked descending turn away from his wingman. His wingman followed, trying to maintain formation integrity. In the turn, John looked down and saw the donut shaped cloud of smoke from a missile launch and a missile the size of a telephone pole headed straight for them.

"Hank nine o'clock low!!...pull hard!!" John radioed through clenched teeth.

The primary evasive maneuver when there's a lock-on and launch is a hard turn away from the path of the missile, hard enough to get the mechanical gyros in the missile's guidance system to tumble, so it can't track its target. Then you pray it doesn't detonate close enough to do any major damage. This was another SA6 and it passed 50 feet away from the belly of the trailing F-4C, its proximity fuse detonating the war head, tossing both aircraft on the resulting shock wave.

All the enunciator panels in Hank and Sandy's aircraft were lit up again with the audio warnings blaring. Their right engine flamed out with a compressor stall and the left engine was surging, probably from ingesting debris. Hank rolled the plane level and pulled the running engine back to idle so it wouldn't come apart. There was smoke in the cockpit and both crewmen went to 100% oxygen.

"Red lead, we've got problems!" Hank blasted over the airwaves.

"Roger that, Hank. I'm at your five o'clock high. You've lost a good chunk of your right wing outbound of the hinge, but I think you're flyable. I'll have a look underneath, just hold it steady. We'll handle the radios."

As Red Lead surveyed the damage from the outside, Hank and Sandy were sweating blood inside the cockpit running through their emergency checklists, trying to restart the right engine, and clearing the smoke from the cockpit. Dan was on the radios alerting Search and Rescue and letting Mission Control know where the enemy threat was, so a mission could be launched against it.

"OK, Hank, your underside has a lot of small holes and tears, but nothing major. Looks like the holes in the fuel cells have self sealed, leakage looks minimal."

"Roger that, John, it doesn't look good. I don't think we'll get the right engine re-started. We may need to shut down the left engine, all the gauges are headed south."

"Ah...roger that. Stand by."

"Shit!" John said over the intercom. "They can't bail out here. There's no way rescue can get to them before the North Vietnamese pick them up. Talk to rescue and see what our options are." Too many aviators had survived similar emergencies, only to rot away in some NV or VC prison camp...or worse.

Hank came up on the flight's discreet frequency, "John, we're going to have to shut down the left engine, it's about to come apart".

"Roger that, we've got rescue working." John observed the deployment of their SCRAM, an impeller that drops into the air stream to turn a hydraulic pump, supplying hydraulic pressure to keep the flight controls working when both engines are dead. The flight was descending through

8,000 feet into a narrow river valley running southwest away from the coast. An F-4C with two dead engines doesn't glide very far.

It seemed an interminable length of time before Dan came back up on the discreet frequency again, "Hank, rescue can't do anything unless you can make it to the coast and get 'feet wet'. They have two Jollies and a Hercules on station east of Hyphong that they're vectoring toward us."

There was a prolonged silence...then Hank came back on the radio.

"John, stick around as long as you can, we'll come up on Guard channel as soon as we're on the ground." It was standard procedure for the flight to loiter over a downed wingman for as long as possible to act as radio relay, coordinate any firepower available to suppress enemy attempts to kill or capture the crew, and take a final fix on their last known position or direction of movement, in the event a rescue attempt became possible later.

The resignation in Hank's voice spurred John to action. "Hank, delay your ejection another 1000 feet. I'm going to get you out of here, if I have to carry you on my back." And that's basically what John did.

Red Lead dropped from his trailing ten o'clock high position down to a position just below the engine exhausts of his crippled wingman and had them lower their tail hook. He caught the tail hook in the cooling scoop on the forward right side of his nose, and pushed forward on the power until his canopy bow was crammed up under the dead engines. On the first attempt, the pair started bucking like a mechanical bull in a Texas dance hall, and John had to back away.

"Hank, give me ten degree flaps and when you feel me applying power, trim it slightly nose up." John re-assumed the position and advanced to full military power. This time it worked. The locked pair was porposing moderately, but quickly began picking up airspeed. John carefully raised the throttles, one at a time, up over the ramp into minimum afterburner, then slowly pushed both throttles forward all the way to the firewall for maximum power. He called his wingman for more nose up trim, and the pair began to rise, in a slow wallowing climb. They worked their way out of the south end of the valley and made a shallow, lazy turn east toward the South China Sea...that was the end of Act One.

Dan was on the radios trying to coordinate Act Two. John's stunt was unprecedented, and they weren't sure what to do next. With the fuel consumption in full afterburner, pushing a dead aircraft, they weren't sure they could even make it to the coast. Now they had two planes and four crewmen in jeopardy; Mission Control was shitting bricks.

They made it to the coast. The two HH-53 Jolly Green Giant helicopters with an HC-130 Hercules control ship circling overhead were already on station awaiting their arrived. Three miles out, over a relatively calm sea, John throttled back and dropped his speed brakes to disengage the two F-4Cs, tearing away the radome cover on the nose of his aircraft in the process. Hank and Sandy initiated their ejection sequence without difficulty...two good chutes. Rescue parachute jumpers were being dropped in the water near them almost before their feet were wet.

By now Red Lead was well into fuel reserves and the 'fuel low' lights were on, they had already silenced the audio alarms. Dan was again on the radios coordinating options. A KC-135 tanker, normally posted fifty miles out to sea farther south, had been vectored north and dropped from its normal 20,000 foot station down to 10,000 feet. John was already on an intercept heading. Seven minutes later the tanker was climbing back toward the south with a damage F-4C hanging off its fuel pipe...end of Act Two.

Hank found John and Dan at the bar. Dan was white as a sheet and already drunk. John had his face buried in a hot towel with one of the bar girls massaging his neck and shoulders, flight suit opened to the waist. This was the standard after mission routine for most of the aircrews stationed at Udorn. After landing, all four crewmen had been separated for post-flight debriefing, urine and blood tests, and a physical, which were normal procedures following an accident or incident where there'd been a loss of an aircraft or a life.

Hank and John eventually carried Dan back to his 'hooch' and spent the rest of the night nursing a bottle of bourbon by the pool, talking about every fear or aspiration either of them had ever had. In those hours they became brothers, in a way that only war or crisis brings men together, a deep personal bond that would have lasted a life time.

Two months later, Hank and Sandy didn't come back from a mission. It would be nineteen years before a team trying to resolve missing in action cases returned from a recently discovered crash site just inside the Cambodia border with a few bone fragments and the decals identifying Hank and Sandy's aircraft, finally closing a chapter in John's life.

***

(Continued)